CONTENT

C000318497

CHOICE

Jason Allen-Paisant • *Self-Portrait as Othello* • Carcanet

RECOMMENDATIONS

Liz Berry • *The Home Child* • Chatto & Windus
Sarala Estruch • *After All We Have Travelled* • Nine Arches Press
Will Harris • *Brother Poem* • Granta
Carole Satyamurti • *The Hopeful Hat* • Bloodaxe Books

SPECIAL COMMENDATION

Peter Bennet • *Nayler & Folly Wood* • Bloodaxe Books

TRANSLATION CHOICE

Agnès Agboton • *Voice of the Two Shores* • Flipped Eye Publishing
Translated by Lawrence Schimel

PAMPHLET CHOICE

Ellora Sutton • *Antonyms for Burial* • Fourteen Poems

Poetry Book Society

CHOICE SELECTORS RECOMMENDATION SPECIAL COMMENDATION	JO CLEMENT & ROY McFARLANE
TRANSLATION SELECTOR	HARRY JOSEPHINE GILES
PAMPHLET SELECTORS	NINA MINGYA POWLES & ARJI MANUELPILLAI
CONTRIBUTORS	SOPHIE O'NEILL MEGAN ROBSON LEDBURY CRITICS
EDITORIAL & DESIGN	ALICE KATE MULLEN

Poetry Book Society Memberships

Choice

4 Books a Year: 4 Choice books & 4 *Bulletins* (UK £65, Europe £85, ROW £120)

World

8 Books: 4 Choices, 4 Translation books & 4 *Bulletins* (£98, £160, £190)

Complete

24 Books: 4 Choices, 16 Recommendations, 4 Translations & 4 *Bulletins* (£230, £290, £360)

Single copies of the *Bulletin* £9.99

Cover Artwork *Kuruka* by Patrick Dougher www.godbodyart.com @patrickdougher
Copyright Poetry Book Society and contributors. All rights reserved.
ISBN 9781913129439   ISSN 0551-1690

Poetry Book Society | Milburn House | Dean Street | Newcastle upon Tyne | NE1 1LF
0191 230 8100 | enquiries@poetrybooksociety.co.uk

WWW.POETRYBOOKS.CO.UK

LETTER FROM THE PBS

Exciting times at Poetry Book Society HQ, Alice our wonderful PBS Manager has been part of the British Council sponsored International Publishing Fellowship in India. This included a January trip to Jaipur Literature Festival where she represented the PBS at Jaipur BookMark. We are hopeful that one of the outcomes of the trip will be a one-off India focused publication for members and the wider poetry readership. Watch this space! If you'd like something to pique your interest in poetry from India, as part of this fellowship we hosted a brilliant online event at Kolkata's International Poetry Festival, featuring recent Choice Sandeep Parmar which is now available to view on our website.

Back to the Spring 2023 selections. No difficult second book here, three of the selections are much anticipated second collections from Jason Allen-Paisant, this season's Choice, Liz Berry and Will Harris. These are accompanied by Sarala Estruch's debut and a posthumous collection from Carole Satyamurti. I was particularly struck by the Translation Choice *Voice of the Two Shores* from Agnès Agboton which is presented in three languages: the original Gun (a language of Benin) translated by the poet into Spanish then translated by Lawrence Schimel into English – what a journey!

I can't write about all the books, the selectors and poets do a much better job. It's an intriguing group of selections and reviewed titles. We expect many members will order up copies and use their 25% member discount wisely. I certainly have them all on my shelf now!

Many congratulations to our Metro Poetry Prize winner J.E. Neary and runners-up Susan Shepherd, Helen Kay and Jane Burn. You can read their winning poems on display at Longbenton Metro station. Come March in Newcastle we also have a brilliant event in partnership with Newcastle Centre for the Literary Arts featuring the last two Choice poets, Jason Allen-Paisant and Safiya Kamaria Kinshasa. Safiya will combine poetry and dance which promises to be a wonderful experience. Thanks as always for your support, we really appreciate our PBS members and look forward to arranging more in-person events in the future where we can actually meet face to face.

SOPHIE O'NEILL
PBS & INPRESS DIRECTOR

JASON ALLEN-PAISANT

Jason Allen-Paisant is a poet and academic from Jamaica. He holds a DPhil in Medieval and Modern Languages from the University of Oxford and works as a senior lecturer in Critical Theory and Creative Writing at the University of Manchester. He's the author of two poetry collections *Thinking with Trees* (Carcanet Press, 2021), winner of the 2022 OCM Bocas Prize for poetry, and *Self-Portrait as Othello* (Carcanet Press, 2023). His monograph *Engagements with Aimé Césaire* will be published by Oxford University Press in 2023, and his non-fiction book *Scanning the Bush* will be out with Hutchinson Heinemann in 2024. He lives in Leeds with his wife and two children.

SELF-PORTRAIT AS OTHELLO

CARCANET | £12.99 | PBS PRICE   £9.75

Afropean was a book by Johny Pitts, a discourse about being wholly black in a European landscape. In *Self-Portrait as Othello*, we continue this conversation, embarking on a journey across Europe, interspersed with hauntings, absent fathers, and a mother passing away.

> Your silence is a haunting, brothers are wanting,
> people are waiting to hear. I conjure you
> furiously.

Allen-Paisant conjures up the character of Othello, who steps out of Shakespeare's imagination and embodies the narrator of these poems, as he walks into clubs and theatres and along the streets of Paris, Prague and Oxford. If I were to take inspiration from Mutabaruka's song *Gimmie Mi Dis Gimmie Mi Dat*, I would say "gimmie mi back, Otello who you lambast and abuse, mek mi gee him dignity and life infused."

Holding *Les Fleurs du Mal* by Charles Baudelaire in his hands, we experience alienation at the heart of the city. Another act of alienation is language but Allen-Paisant sets us free, speaking in tongues, patois, French and English; a hunger for an alternative narrative (outside the European gaze) for stories and the liquid of language:

> show me the hidden side of the script I want
> the kind of life that can be read
> not piddling paltry mooching along instead
> why do I always have to be translated

Where *Thinking with Trees* was an exploration of Black identity and its connection to the environment, *Self-Portrait as Othello* moves from the rural to the Metropole. In 'Place De La Nation' we're reminded that the act of being, of existing, is often a dangerous act for Black bodies, as the narrator sees:

> ...two beautiful dark-skinned children
> just innocently sitting on a bench waiting,
> not bothering anyone, just waiting &
> you want to weep because they are so beautiful
>
> and nobody should be wrong to be
> so beautiful in this world

ROY McFARLANE

JASON ALLEN-PAISANT

Self-Portrait as Othello is a poetic memoir. It's also a lyric exploration of the dramas of migration and border crossings. The questions I put to Shakespeare's Othello come from the recognition of a protagonist who must contend with the pain of leaving and arriving. One of the things that intrigued me was the realisation that, if Othello came from elsewhere, he must have had another language. Where did that language sit in Shakespeare's imagination? What happens when I imagine Othello with all the density of a mother tongue that shaped him, outside the world of the Shakespearean text? Othello is, of course, a fictional character, but he's also very real – he represents a real structure of feeling. As I reflected on crossings, and leavings, there was a slight slippage into thinking about the racialised immigrant whose complexity gets flattened out in the process of arriving, becoming, and integrating. Othello threw up the possibility of a lyric examination of the dark-skinned male body as it negotiates the realities of leaving and arriving in a framework of difference and othering.

Given the dearth of archival representations of African lives in Renaissance Venice, I wanted to move physically towards Othello by visiting that city; I did so twice. In Venice, I observed the lives of African immigrants and stood for hours looking at paintings in the Gallerie dell'Accademia. What struck me in paintings by Veronese, Titian, and others, were their portrayals of African characters; these felt like a different history of representation of the Black body, a complex, if ambiguous one. The experiences in Venice brought a particular energy to the book and a way of understanding what was really driving me, i.e., the visual imagination around the Black male body. I was interested in narratives that upend stereotypes – as I realised, this sometimes meant inventing them. The urge of invention and self-invention explains my fascination with the paintings of Kehinde Wiley. One of them *Willem van Heythuysen* is the cover image of my book. The model in this painting is a shape-shifter, just like my Othello. He (my Othello) is a liminal figure. His playful slipperiness in language and in social space is an expression of his fluidity.

JASON RECOMMENDS

Layli Long Soldier, *Whereas* (Graywolf Press); Billy-Ray Belcourt, *A History of My Brief Body* (Two Dollar Radio); Dionne Brand, *Nomenclature: New and Collected Poems* (Duke University Press); Safiya Kamaria Kinshasa, *Cane, Corn, and Gully* (Out-spoken Press); Bhanu Kapil, *How to Wash a Heart* (Pavilion); Lorna Goodison, *Collected Poems* (Carcanet); Jean 'Binta' Breeze, *Third World Girl* (Bloodaxe); Forrest Gander, *Your Nearness* (Arc Publications); Kim Hyesoon, *Autobiography of Death* (W.W. Norton); Natalie Diaz, *Postcolonial Love Poem* (Faber); Fran Lock, *White/ Other* (the87press).

SELF-PORTRAIT AS OTHELLO II

The Black body is signed as physically and psychically open space... A space not simply owned by those who embody it but constructed and occupied by other embodiments. Inhabiting it is a domestic, hemispheric... transatlantic... international pastime. There is a playing around in it.
- Dionne Brand, *A Map to the Door of No Return*

You left home for a wandering lust for pain
   had driven you to the edge of yourself & wanting
to open the windows of life you decided to migrate to this
   country. You came for a different sound

the quaintness of gestures of faces & food. New tongues
   are something like trophies *faccia* faces *façades...*
The façade hides things you like this each new word
   an erotic death your language grows with buried things

What does it mean to be *far more fair than black?*
   Education speech dress learning. You have the brawn
of an intellectual rude boy sturdier in brain-work
   than in war. Know streets and livity talk Shakespeare

Baudelaire Dante and Nietzsche talk sound system. What actually
   is the language of where you're from? It's that familiarity
with rough life that eye of struggle that smell of fight
   hardness of speech a coming up vibe Oxford and all

that she likes so invites you to visit at Christmas three whole days
   with family and one party to the next but they think
it's going to pass this fascination with the dark-skinned boy surely
   she'll come around find someone of her kind *when she is sated.*

PUNTED DOWN THE CHERWELL

If my mother had told me a white man
would serve you I would have said

you lie serve you over there
that you would be over the white man
in his own country

Oh colonial in defeat
image of centuries swallowed
look

Look at them teeth how they white
as I sail down the river Cherwell
with a white man punting my punt

LIZ BERRY

Liz Berry's debut collection *Black Country*, "a sooty, soaring hymn to her native West Midlands" (*Guardian*), won a Somerset Maugham Award, the Geoffrey Faber Memorial Prize, and the Forward Prize for Best First Collection. Her pamphlet *The Republic of Motherhood* was a Poetry Book Society Pamphlet Choice and the title poem won the Forward Prize for Best Single Poem in 2018. In *The Home Child*, a novel in verse, she reimagines the story of her great-aunt Eliza Showell, one of the many children forcibly emigrated to Canada as part of the British Child Migrant schemes.

RECOMMENDATION

THE HOME CHILD

CHATTO & WINDUS | £14.99 | PBS PRICE £11.25

Few can master the verse novel as Liz Berry has in *The Home Child*. Her trademark Ovidian knack for the shape-shifty poem kicks a hoof clean through the page. Unseating our trust in the epistolic and reportage modes she employs, Berry's regional tongue is an instrument for protest through which we discover the most divine pleasures:

> so I hold out my ond (hand)
> til he takes it and kisses the palm
> like he's eating sugar from it

At 12 years old Eliza Showell, Liz Berry's great-aunt, was sent to Canada. Britain shipped over one hundred and fifty thousand so-called Home Children to colonies across the globe between the 1860s and 1970s. Most were forced into exploitative agricultural and domestic labour. Some found kind homes.

> Description: Nice bright-looking girl, rather short.
> To be taken in.

Torn from the Black Country's impoverished and industrial Bilston slums, Eliza arrives in Cape Breton's stark rural snows. Berry's cant-rich dialect studs this unfamiliar territory – lands stolen from its indigenous Unama'ki people – with secret "bibbles" and "tranklements". A pair of stand-out poems titled 'They Say' catalogue the cruelties suffered by Home Children through their testimony, to reveal that malnourishment, rape and beatings happened as routinely as Sunday school prayer.

The Home Child is a songbook of resistance. When Eliza meets a Glaswegian Home Boy, the collection shifts tonally from claustrophobic servitude to the freedom of self-discovery. Berry's folkloric lyricism thrums with the pentatonic energy of deep Southern blues:

> Fifteen last week, he's lonesome and whip-thin,
> no past, no home, he's lonesome and whip-thin,
> sweet Jesus, the force of her tenderness cursed him.

In this paean to displaced identity and Northern English dialect, *wum*, meaning home, repeats throughout. Womb, its ear-rhyme, echoes, as if in ultrasound: full of a furious longing for a loved, lost family and the cruellest motherland.

JO CLEMENT

| SELECTOR'S COMMENT

LIZ BERRY

The Home Child is a novel in verse that reimagines the story of my great-aunt Eliza Showell. In 1908, aged twelve and newly orphaned, Eliza was sent from a children's home in Birmingham to work in indentured service in rural Nova Scotia. She never returned to England or saw her brothers again. Eliza was a "Home Child", one of over 100,000 poor and vulnerable children who were forcibly migrated to Canada between the 1860s and 1960s as part of the disastrous British Child Migrant schemes.

I first discovered Eliza's story when I was setting off on my own journey to Nova Scotia. I was on a literary pilgrimage to Green Gables, home of the eponymous Anne, another twelve-year old orphan and my girlhood heroine. In L.M. Montgomery's novels, Anne – a Canadian – becomes beloved in a way Home Children seldom were. Though born poor and exploited, she remains full of spirit and wonder, and the world falls in love with her. Pulled from the hidden branches of our family tree, Eliza's story felt like a shadow to Anne's. Combing through the records from her children's home and the few traces of her life left, I found the terrible stigma and powerlessness of poverty but also the profound capacity humans have for love and survival even when the world is very cold to them. Laying wildflowers on Eliza's small grave in Cape Breton, I knew I wanted to bring her story – and those of Home Children like her – to the light.

I've tried to tell Eliza's story with the utmost care and respect. When writing, I imagined holding her as gently as I hold my own sons. I changed many details and invented many things but tried to keep the heart of the story true. I'm grateful to the brave Home Children who shared their experiences through letters, interviews and books as their first hand accounts were integral to my imagining of Eliza's life. I hope *The Home Child* will be a pleasure to read, poems which tell a tender story. As the wild violets sing to Eliza: "Home's not a place, you must believe this / but one who names you and means beloved."

LIZ RECOMMENDS

When I was writing *The Home Child* I asked poets to tell me about the verse novels and long poetic sequences they loved. Here are some of my favourites: *Thomas and Beulah* by Rita Dove (Carnegie Mellon); *The Adoption Papers* by Jackie Kay (Bloodaxe Books); *Autobiography in Red* by Anne Carson (Cape); *Surge* by Jay Bernard (Chatto & Windus); *Fairoz* by Moniza Alvi (Bloodaxe); *Chan* by Hannah Lowe (Bloodaxe); *Vertigo & Ghost* by Fiona Benson (Cape); *The Long Take* by Robin Robertson (Picador); *Lost City* by Roz Goddard (Emma Press) and *Deaf Republic* by Ilya Kaminsky (Faber).

Happiness is a wind
that whistles straight through

Jacket illustration © Gemma Trickey

OUT WEST

The land swallowed them,
guttled them, spat out their dreams,
broke their bones with its wintery teeth, its frozen farms,
gobbled them into the loam like bad seeds
and let the worms comfort them;
there, inspite the drought and the flood,
the hostile roots of the spruce,
the teeth of voles in the autumn mulch,
their green shoots pushed up
into the wild blue, to the love of the sun.
Walk across the hills of Whycocomagh
when the light near blinds you
and you will see them in the furrows,
in the heartsore violets, the shivering pines.

Image: Alan Howard

SARALA ESTRUCH

Sarala Estruch is a British writer, poet, and researcher. *After All We Have Travelled* is her debut full-length poetry collection. Her pamphlet *Say* (flipped eye, 2021) was a Poetry School Book of The Year. A finalist of the Primers mentorship scheme and a fellow of the Ledbury Poetry Critics programme, her poetry, creative non-fiction, and reviews have been widely published including in *The Poetry Review, Wasafiri,* and *The Guardian,* and featured on BBC Radio 3's *The Verb.* Sarala is currently a doctoral candidate at the University of Liverpool, where she is a recipient of the JIC Davies Studentship. She lives in London.

AFTER ALL WE HAVE TRAVELLED

NINE ARCHES PRESS | £10.99 | PBS PRICE £8.25

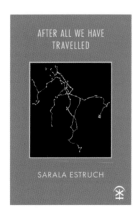

"And after the fire a still small voice," Elijah wrote in the *Bible* in reference to finding a deity in the mouth of a cave rather than in the volcano. Similarly, in Sarala Estruch's debut, we find mighty utterance in the essence of stillness, the hush of recollections, memories and stories. Estruch begins with 'On Sound' a declaration that all sounds can be heard however, small and indifferent:

> crush / reverberates
> indefinitely / at a
> frequency / our ears
> cannot touch / but
> the body / hears

There's a trauma and a reckoning with a past, especially the loss of her father. The narrator ventures into the silence, the abyss, using different forms from free verse to Ghazals. I love Estruch's use of the forward slash, like Natalie Diaz she "make(s) the readers' eyes uncomfortable... express(ing) the disjointed, jagged experience".

We witness the love of an interracial couple and the child they bring into this world and the effects it has on several generations before and after. Photographs, clothing, letters and dreams are used to evoke moments. 'Starting from a Dream, 1983' is a poem of forbode, a confluence of two thoughts that become one, an echo of duality through the collection.

Estruch continues to play with space, poems are shaped by a pressured silence, fracturing sentences, couplets have two meanings, columns of poems speak to each other on the page, some of it reflecting the way memory can be fractured. In others there's a desire to be seen, whilst in 'Freight', there is an inner conversation and the hidden journey.

> me 'pretty'.
> My chameleon skin
> (platinum in snow
>
> bronze in sun) meant
> 'passing' was a place to hide

There's nothing hidden in this collection, narratives of Partition and empire, historical and interpersonal traumas are brought to light, as in the words of Raymond Antrobus "because grief never leaves, it just changes shape".

ROY McFARLANE

| SELECTOR'S COMMENT

SARALA ESTRUCH

After All We Have Travelled began as a novel. In 2016, I read Bhanu Kapil's *The Vertical Interrogation of Strangers* and was struck by the energy and beautiful subversiveness of its hybrid prose-poetry style as well as its portrayal and examination of the complexities of love, betrayal, grief, itinerancy and (un)belonging, intergenerational and (inter)national traumas, and the reverberations of colonialism and empire. Inspired, and wanting to explore the same themes, I started to write a lyrical novel, which was a reimagining of my parents' relationship (how they came together and how they separated), as well as an exploration, more widely, of the legacies of colonialism and imperialism.

I never completed that novel, possibly because what interested me most in telling this story was not narrative progression but language, specifically language's ability and inability to convey and probe the complexities of human psychology and emotion. Instead, the story began to emerge in the shape of discrete poems, which were nevertheless interlinked by the themes and subjects I have already described.

After All We Have Travelled was written over the course of six or so years, and the central question I kept returning to was: What are the things that separate us from ourselves and each other? The book explores man-made divisions: racism, nationalism and xenophobia, as well as separation along cultural and religious lines, from concrete conceptions of division, like national and geographic borders, to metaphysical separations, such as death, time, and memory.

This book is an exploration of mixed-race, mixed-heritage, and diasporic identities – particularly the pressures to claim one race or cultural heritage over another – and is in conversation with the rich and growing body of literature on mixed-race and diasporic identities, including Sarah Howe's *Loop of Jade* and Will Harris' *RENDANG*.

SARALA RECOMMENDS

All works by Audre Lorde, Lucille Clifton, Bhanu Kapil, Sandeep Parmar, and Claudia Rankine. Sarah Howe, *Loop of Jade* (Chatto); Will Harris, *RENDANG* (Granta); Kayo Chingonyi, *Kumukanda* (Chatto); Ocean Vuong, *Night Sky with Exit Wounds* (Cape); Marie Howe, *What the Living Do* (W.W. Norton); Hannah Lowe, *Chick* (Bloodaxe) and *Chan* (Bloodaxe); Emily Berry, *Stranger, Baby* (Faber); Moniza Alvi, *At the Time of Partition* (Bloodaxe); Fatimah Asghar, *If They Come For Us* (Corsair); Shivanee Ramlochan, *Everyone Knows I Am A Haunting* (Peepal Tree Press); Layli Long Soldier, *Whereas* (Picador).

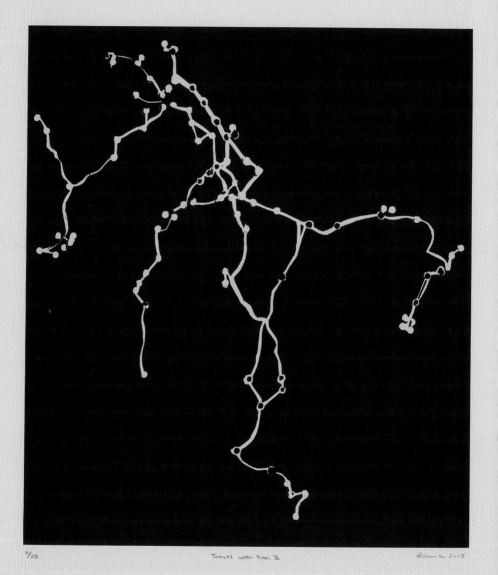

11/25   Travel with Rani II   Zarina 2008

Image: *Travel with Rani II*, 2008 © Zarina; courtesy of the artist and Luhring Augustine, New York.
Photo: Farzad Owrang.

VAISAKHI, *VAISAKHI*

*Vaisakhi is a spring festival celebrated throughout India and the world.
Britain still hasn't formally apologised for the Jallianwala Bagh massacre
which took place in Amritsar on Vaisakhi in 1919.*

14 April 2019   *13 April 1919*

On the morning of Vaisakhi   *On the morning of Vaisakhi*
we rise and, after breakfast,   *we rise and, after breakfast,*
dress our heads in cotton cloth   *dress in our finest, travel to*
climb the white stone staircase   *Jallianwala Bagh and gather*
to Grandfather's prayer room   *with family and friends*

On the roof, we remove   *In full sunlight, we sit*
our shoes and step into   *on packed earth, spread*
the glass-panelled room   *the cloth, lay out food*
bowing before the sacred book   *We thank God for the meal*
as Uncle has shown us   *bring rice and dal to our mouths*

Grandfather is already there   *The soldiers are already there:*
sat behind the Guru Granth Sahib   *standing on the mount, guns raised*
draped in gold gossamer   *Bullets burst Bodies tumble*
he pulls away The children watch   *to the earth The children watch*
in silence The children wait   *in silence The children wait*

Grandfather opens the book   *Then they run, we all run –*
at random, begins to read and   *there is nowhere to go Bullets*
we listen, understanding not   *pummelling the single exit*
with our ears but with our hearts: *which is also the single entrance*
a lord's prayer on this auspicious day   *Some of us jump into the well –*

When he is finished, he reads   *We who survive utter prayers*
another prayer just for us   *for those we lost The time*
which he translates line by line   *has passed for screaming; the time*
thanking God for our safe arrival   *is ripe for grieving For apology*
blessing our golden lives   *Atonement Healing*

SARALA ESTRUCH

21

Image: Matthew Thompson

WILL HARRIS

Will Harris is the author of *RENDANG* (2020),
which was shortlisted for the T.S. Eliot Prize and
won the Forward Prize for Best First Collection. He
has collaborated with the artist Aisha Farr, and helps
facilitate the Southbank New Poets Collective. He
co-translated Habib Tengour's *Consolatio* with Delaina
Haslam in 2022. He works in extra care homes in
Tower Hamlets as an activity worker, and is currently
working on a project based around care and artmaking.

BROTHER POEM

GRANTA | £10.99 | PBS PRICE £8.25

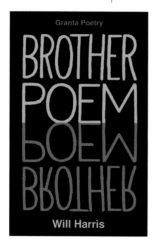

Brother Poem slides with ease between art-house parties, steamy chicken shops and anxiety dreams. In the spirit of Stuart Hall, this hotly anticipated follow-up to *RENDANG* challenges fixed notions of race through lived experiences of Chinese-Indonesian-British ethnicity and the trading language Bahasa: "no one asked how my / speech and face related". An epigraph by Anna Akhmatova whispers throughout: "I am hushed, as if I'd lost a brother". Culminating in the long title poem, this two-part sequence tenderly grapples with sibling loss:

> I knew
> you must be listening
> but you wouldn't speak

Like the poet's mother tongue, the Brother figure becomes present through his absence. But the conceit of this elegy is evident in Akhmatova's "as if". Harris is an only child:

> Brother
> it's a funny
> word to say or
> to address to you as if
> you were here...

Those without imaginations might consider this an "awkward / postscript" but it is the power of this collection. The fictive Brother becomes the speaker's uncanny avatar, an elusive and yet persistent force: "What will I do / in the future / Use I or him / when I mean you"? With echoes of Whitman's "multitudes", Harris makes sincere dialogue against the notion of a "true" or "frozen" self. We become many different selves across the course of our lives and these poems celebrate the many ideas, or so-called "waiting Brother(s)" that we might write.

Illustrated with family photographs and alert with a Saussurean distrust of language, *Brother Poem* is a surreal collection in which people and history are as constructed as artificial lakes and the Aldi veg aisle. Turning I.D. cards and bubble tea into memorable "events in language", Harris interrogates the confessional lyric mode with sincere wit and dolefully plays with the "I-not-I":

> behind whose silence
> crackles the poem

WILL HARRIS

Brother Poem is made up of thirteen poems, a series of notes to those poems, and a final poem. Half of the book's length is taken up with a sequence called 'Brother Poem'; the brother figure also appears in three poems in the first section. "Brother figure" because the brother is never named. Mostly he is a silent addressee, a "you" who won't talk back. He carries the weight of implied kinship, of family elsewhere, of family that never existed but is nevertheless longed for and mourned (speculatively, impossibly).

> You were my brother. We were
> events in language...

I started writing the poems four years ago. I was trying to imagine how I'd think about my childhood if I'd had a brother (I'm an only child). I started writing because I was lonely as a child. I liked the ambiguity of "you". When I wrote to someone called "you" it didn't matter if I got a response; it happens. Trying to understand the book after the fact, I've thought of it in terms of the horizontal axis: the plane of kinship, of what's next to you. The book exists, for me, on that hopeful axis, a way of using poetry to simulate (model) kinship, to hear myself speaking to someone who knows me, or wants to. Poetry like the weather.

> ...A mode of talking through, of lightness
> over meals. As weather makes contact with the ground, snow grains
> spilling through our hands assuming resistance, we hear
> ourselves as we exist, without any principle but that which reaches
> beyond speech, because the sky surrounds us falling upwards.

WILL RECOMMENDS

Joe recommended Celan this year and I finally read him and can't get over 'Over wine and lostness' from *Die Niemandsrose*. Sophie recommended John James two years ago and I still think of his 'Poem Beginning with a Line of Andrew Crozier' and "the poetry of kindred". Recent books I've loved include Aurelia Guo's *World of Interiors* and Sandeep Parmar's *Faust*. The way Parmar breaks images across lines – enacting the politically embodied movement of thought – is incredible. I work in Tower Hamlets and Stephen Watts's *Journeys Across Breath* and *Republic of Dogs/Republic of Birds* have also provided a language for movement, and a rhythm adequate to the places and people of East London, as deformed by capital. I also read Susan Stewart's *Letter on Sound* and loved her reading of G.M. Hopkins' letters to Baillie on instress and inscape, and the interlinking of form and experience.

I RECOMMENDATION

BROTHER POEM

Brother
it's a funny
word to say or
to address to you as if
you were here because if you were
I wouldn't be saying it that's what's funny

Brother
more a question
than a name with the
implication being do you have a brother
what does your brother do where is your brother

Brother
a frozen word
like being on the other
side of a locked door one of
those walk-in freezers where they
hang big slabs of meat *brrrrr* I'm outside
standing by the airtight door whispering through
each steel hinge what was that you'll have to speak up
I can't hear a word you're saying no I can't hear anything

BROTHER
　　BROTHER
　　　　BROTH–
before I knew your
　　face or name
I saw the moons
　　　of spring
　　fatal　moons
which for days
　　on end became
whatever was most
　　　unkind till
　　in a voice so
　　　in a shapeless
flame an image
　　in excelsis came
and clear enough
　　to make the old
　　　world groan
there you were
　　open and sublime
　　a bundle
of saliva waiting
　　to be kissed

Image: Martin Wilkinson

CAROLE SATYAMURTI

Carole Satyamurti (1939-2019) was a poet and sociologist. For many years she taught at the Tavistock Clinic, where her main academic interest was in the relevance of psychoanalytic ideas to an understanding of the stories people tell about themselves, whether in formal autobiography or in social encounters. She co-edited *Acquainted with the Night: psychoanalysis and the poetic imagination* (Karnac, 2003). She won the National Poetry Competition in 1986, and a Cholmondeley Award in 2000. Her *Selected Poems* (Oxford University Press, 1998) was reissued by Bloodaxe Books in 2000. Her *Mahabharata: A Modern Retelling* (W.W. Norton, 2015) was joint winner of the inaugural Roehampton Poetry Prize. Her Bloodaxe retrospective *Stitching the Dark: New & Selected Poems* (2005) drew on five collections: *Broken Moon* (1987), *Changing the Subject* (1990), *Striking Distance* (1994), *Love and Variations* (2000), and *Stitching the Dark* (2005). Two of these were Poetry Book Society Recommendations. This was followed by *Countdown* (2011) and her final collection *The Hopeful Hat* which has been published posthumously.

THE HOPEFUL HAT

BLOODAXE BOOKS | £10.99 | PBS PRICE £8.25

Carole Satyamurti

THE HOPEFUL HAT

POETRY BOOK SOCIETY RECOMMENDATION

In 'The Seventh Seal' the protagonist plays a game of chess with Death to delay the inevitable, a knight returning from the Crusade in the time of the Black Plague making his way home. In the opening poem 'The Hopeful Hat', the narrator sees a dishevelled woman at a bus stop, playing a recorder, and comes across her several times in the day.

> Her one hopeless note follows me home,
> and here I write my shabby conscience out.

In this collection, this is not a delaying of the inevitable and certainly more than a shabby conscience but a writing into the impermanence of it all. Satyamurti without voice (due to laryngeal cancer) and with terminal cancer, speaks aloud across the pages. She "invites you to consider now, and now, / the quiddity of all that is." Divided in four sections Satyamurti is lyrical and at her best when speaking of the power of the tongue and the loss of voice. In 'Voicing the Void' and in 'Glossal' we hear the power of the tongue...

> of this most potent sixty grams of flesh –
> this truth-teller, this incendiary organ,
> this evolutionary achievement
> as vital to the human core of us
> as the heart is – can shift the world

The narrator recollects love affairs, a grand piano finding its voice again, poems of social injustice and preparing for bin collections on Wednesdays. Full of warmth and awareness of a life lived well, she declares in 'Shoreline':

> You approach the sea like a homecoming:
> Your vast origin; your (dis)solution.
>
> You are the breather and the breathed.
> The question and the questioner.

I can't help but imagine that Satyamurti is playing with E.B. White's quote "Hang on to your hat. Hang on to your hope. And wind the clock, for tomorrow is another day." Here she climbs that Victorian clock and in her way winds back time, whilst singing "Mr Sandman... Show me the way to go home".

ROY McFARLANE

SELECTOR'S COMMENT

CAROLE SATYAMURTI: A TRIBUTE

My mother, Carole Satyamurti, died in University College Hospital, London on 13th August 2019, sooner than expected after receiving a diagnosis of terminal cancer. Many conversations were left un-had, including about the poems contained in this collection. She had been working on it for some time but had not yet submitted it to her publisher or given any other definitive indication that she considered the work finished. Our greatest clue as to her intentions was that the poems were printed out and organised in a way that suggested the shape she envisaged for the book, but with notes making clear that a few of the individual poems were to some extent still work in progress.

The biggest project of Satyamurti's later years was her book *Mahabharata: A Modern Retelling* in which she rendered the vast and vivid Indian epic in 800 pages of what Philip Pullman describes as "supple and muscular verse". The book took some eight years to complete, taking Satyamurti into new and consuming creative territory. After it was finished, I think she felt in some way disconnected from the voice that had breathed the life and meaning into her earlier lyric poems. The poems here mark her re-finding of that voice, familiar from *Countdown* (Bloodaxe, 2011), the last collection published during her lifetime... The question of what a voice can represent is a thread running though Satyamurti's work, often interrogated in particular in relation to poetry itself – how and to what extent poems, and words more broadly, count in the face of suffering and injustice...

> Don't be afraid to make a poem
> raw as sandpaper. And even though
> a million protests, twice as many feet,
> couldn't stop a war, get out there
> with your small voice, your light tread.

By the time of writing the poems in this collection, Satyamurti's interest in the impact and importance of voice and words had been overlaid by a cruel irony. A diagnosis of laryngeal cancer in 2012 had led to the removal of her voice-box and part of her tongue, a loss she bore with courage and resilience... These final poems will inevitably hold particular resonances for those who knew Satyamurti personally, they are about the challenge of facing our mortality, of finding meaning despite (and because of) it; an endeavour which is as quintessentially human as language. In 'Solid', the last poem of this last collection, after describing the permanent nature of atoms Satyamurti leaves us with this characteristically clear-eyed question:

> But there's no denying
> one day you will be dead
> and where do the colours go
> when the carpet fades?

EMMA SATYAMURTI

RECOMMENDATION

...a benighted
sense that, though it's blighted,
the world's still good enough?

Sculpture: Joel Beyney
Photography: Alick Cotterill

VOICING THE VOID

1.

I will never mistake myself
for a decibel
now I can no longer
sing
whistle
play the recorder
shout to save my life.

2.

'One of these days,' said my friend, Raju,
'there'll be an instrument so fine,
so tuned to the subtlest vibrations
pulsing still in the air around us,
that we'll recover the voice of Lord Krishna
exhorting Arjuna to take up arms
on the battlefield of Kurukshetra.'*

He was serious. I thought – how could he,
a man schooled in respect for evidence,
take an ancient text so literally,
be innocent of how a poem can fly
free of facts to furnish the mind's ear
with wonders sprung from imagining?

But now my voice-box has been cut away
I remember Doctor Raju – his conviction,
his devoutly wished for instrument;
imagine my life's piled up utterance
cluttering the ether like space junk,
part of humanity's monstrous din
drowning out the wisdom of the gods.

---

*This refers to an episode in the *Bhagavad Gita*.

CAROLE SATYAMURTI

33

Image: Susan Bennet

PETER BENNET

Peter Bennet taught in secondary and further education, including work with redundant steelworkers following the closure of Consett Steel Works, and spent sixteen years as Tutor Organiser for Northumberland with the Workers' Educational Association. He lived for thirty three years near the Wild Hills o' Wanney in Northumberland, in a cottage associated with the ballad writer James Armstrong, author of *Wanny Blossoms*. He now lives in North Shields. His earlier Bloodaxe retrospective *Border* (2013) included work from *Goblin Lawn* (2005), a Poetry Book Society Recommendation, and *The Glass Swarm* (2008), a Poetry Book Society Choice which was shortlisted for the T.S. Eliot Prize. This was followed by *Mischief* in 2018.

SPECIAL COMMENDATION

NAYLER & FOLLY WOOD

BLOODAXE BOOKS | £14.99 | PBS PRICE £11.25

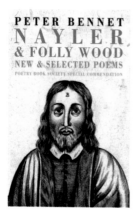

To read *Nayler & Folly Wood* is to know "the hanging dark that cloaks the hillside at your fingers' ends". This arresting retrospective gathers mischievous poems in tune with the metres and matters found on beer-stained slip-songs and in lofty lyrical ballads alike:

> Beneath a bonny rowan tree
> stands Bobby Bendick's mare,
> but Ezra's i' the Ingram Pool
> whilst Bobby droons him theor

Many of these pastorals are meditations on the imagination, sited in meadows where the "ghosts / of mowers move in line like handwriting".

Attentive to folklore, history and craft in equal measure, Peter Bennet charms and unsettles us with wild "wolf-girls" and evil Northumberland bogles. But as his murder ballads reveal: the cruellest beasts take human form.

Spanning over forty years in print, this *New and Selected* includes poems from the T.S. Eliot Prize-shortlisted *Glass Swarm* (2008). 'Nayler' is a bracing new sequence that draws upon significant chapters in the life of the titled Quaker leader, whose:

> verses soothe
> the always present absences
> of those – so many nowadays –
> that need me to remember them

Why might we remember West Yorkshire-born Nayler? On Palm Sunday in 1656, he re-enacted Christ's entry into Jerusalem, by riding into Bristol on horseback to a chorus of hosannas. Soon after, he was arrested, pilloried and his face brutally branded with the letter "B".

Written in Nayler's voice, the lyric takes as its dilemma the perceived criminality of his "horrid blasphemy". This violation of expression invites readers to ask if the "strange acte" of writing or performing a poem could, as with other forms of protest today, also be censored. In these uncertain times, it is comforting to find "poems built like walls" that hold Bennet's lithe, humane and free imagination as "Holy, Holy, Holy" territory.

SELECTOR'S COMMENT

JO CLEMENT

XXIV

The season tilts. Hawthorn and horse chestnut trees
were showing by the end of March. Frogs and toads
have croaked, and swallows scribble air
in order to remind them where they live.
Next, the ash and sycamore and elm, in bud
together, the cuckoo and the nightingale,
and presently the greening of the oak.
My overturning is of boxes. Clutter
bestrews the floor, awaiting aggregation
according to its provenance or function.
Bookshelves have been commissioned. That's a start.
An anchored bicycle for exercise
will stand so I can view Green Rigg,
where lambs lie in clusters on yon bonny brae,
and cloudscapes, ever changing and unchanging,
speeding up into a wide-screen flicker
which is the twentieth-century middle age
I lived through then, and peer at now,
as in a rear-view mirror, darkly trying
to work out how it thinned so soon
into a blurry memory. And I
shall pay attention, James, while pedalling
in sunlight from the glass front door.

AGNÈS AGBOTON

LAWRENCE SCHIMEL

Agnès Agboton is a multilingual author and storyteller residing in Catalonia, Spain. She has published two bilingual books of poetry in Gun and Spanish. Her other titles include an autobiography *Más allá del mar de arena* (*Beyond the Sea of Sand*) and *Na Miton: La mujer en los cuentos y leyendas africanos* (*Na Miton: Women in African Stories and Legends*). She has also written books on African food. She represented Benin at the Poetry Parnassus, at the London 2012 Olympics. English translations of her poems have appeared in *Modern Poetry in Translation* and *New Daughters of Africa*, edited by Margaret Busby.

Lawrence Schimel is a full-time author, writing in both Spanish and English, who has published over 120 books. He is also a prolific literary translator, working into both English and Spanish. He has won the Lambda Literary Award (twice), the Independent Publisher Book Award, a PEN Translates Award three times and a National Endowment for the Arts Translation Fellowship.

| TRANSLATION CHOICE

VOICE OF THE TWO SHORES
AGNÈS AGBOTON

FLIPPED EYE PUBLISHING | £8.99 | PBS PRICE £6.75

AGNÈS AGBOTON
VOICE OF THE TWO SHORES
TRANSLATED BY LAWRENCE SCHIMEL

The body, in Agnès Agboton, is a place of memory, holding both treasure and loss, both trauma and love. The body records lovers, as when "I linger, now, / before the mirror, / searching for the traces of your hands", those same hands which, in another poem, "are measured / against the line of my breasts", but it also holds the weight of painful memories:

> I carry in my entrails the trembling
> of so many smothered gazes.

Though the exhilaration of physical experience runs through these poems, sometimes the body refuses connection: "Do not kiss me; / so much death / has sealed our mouths." The body in these poems often extends out into the natural and social world, and those worlds come into the body. In short, elliptical fragments, "I hear, / this night, / the tree's laughter" and "There are, / in your eyes today, / rumours of rain" – the land speaks, and the body flourishes.

The title's voice of the two shores is the voice of this connection, and also, of course, the voice that speaks across languages. Rarely, this *Collected Poems* is in three languages, republishing Agboton's work in the Gun in which they were written, the Spanish into which she translated them, and the English into which, in collaboration with Agboton, Lawrence Schimel translated the Spanish. This generous presentation allows the reader to follow feelings and memories through the sounds and shapes of each language, and gives a vital prominence to the original language.

The two shores are also now and then: the memory carried in language, in the body, through to the poems of the present. The mystery of how one speaks between languages, between people, of how one translates from the language of memory into the language of speech, runs through the collection: "I wanted to discover the precise centre / where two people / at last meet". In that striving for connection, the joy and sorrow of flesh, itself, offers one answer:

> Everything dances on my skin
> everything dances in my body

HARRY JOSEPHINE GILES

32.

Oxju lèkpo
tó nunkun énin lèmè
bò tó tòjhun xjóxjó lò dji
n'to déé kun.

Zaan enin ...

Todo el océano
está en esos ojos
y en la vieja piragua
navego.

Ese instante ...

The entire ocean
is in those eyes
and in the old canoe
I sail.

That moment ...

ELLORA SUTTON

Ellora Sutton, she/her, is a poet and museum person from Hampshire. She won the 2020 Mslexia Poetry Competition and the inaugural Artlyst Art to Poetry Award and has previously been a young poet in residence at Jane Austen's House. Her work has been published by *The Poetry Review*, *Popshot*, *The North*, and *bath magg*, amongst others, and she reviews poetry for *Mslexia*. She tweets @ellora_sutton.

ANTONYMS FOR BURIAL
FOURTEEN   POEMS | £8.00 |

The best pamphlets are magicians; they have just sixteen to eighteen poems to conjure something magical. Ellora Sutton is a poet doing just that. A poet unafraid of risk, swinging words into cauldrons of wonder with an original and exciting, new voice. This pamphlet will "set the compass of your tongue to salt", this pamphlet is "a broken necked alley leading down to the quay," this pamphlet should be owned by everyone.

From its opening poem you get the feeling Sutton is at home with experimentation. She rolls into clashing form and structure with confidence and verbal dexterity. Some poems are streams of consciousness, darting between thought processes. While others are laid in seemingly endless lists, tourist information notices, scripts, recipes. Any of these styles would not be powerful without Sutton's ability to pull back, to slow us down, to drop into a handful of poems that rely on sparseness, the deep, meditational lines that stick with you for years.

> I read somewhere once
> that this planet can only withstand
> five more atomic bombs
> and this, surely, must be one of them.

The palette of the poems is equally experimental. From moons to toadstools to a crystal ashtray. The sign of its quality is how the writer manages to reimagine poetry clichés into strange, new and brilliant images of wonderment. This talent for imagery is perfectly encapsulated by her 'Self-Portrait as Obscure Facts, a photo series' which throws us in multiple directions. Within that poem she conjures, not only a series of objects that clash, she ties in historical and ethno-botanical responses to the natural world. This is what seems to give it echoes of Rebeccca Tamás, Sarah Howe and Fiona Benson. In the meat of the poem she lists 'Items Anne Sharp received (posthumously) from Jane Austen'. Who else has the guts to roll into such obscure yet somehow exhilarating lists mid-poem.

It feels like something wholly original, a voice in constant celebration of culture and history using the most miraculously beautiful language to take us on a funfair ride around her brain. There is so much magic in this little pamphlet, the only thing I'm wondering now is... when's the collection out?

ARJI MANUELPILLAI & NINA MINGYA POWLES

I SAW A SONG THRUSH

so yellow
so speckled
so quick

it made me want to run through the streets
barefoot knocking on every door saying *Hello I am here
to talk to you today about song thrushes*

I'd never seen one before
I've not seen one since

SPRING BOOK REVIEWS

JOE CARRICK-VARTY: MORE SKY
REVIEWED BY SHALINI SENGUPTA

More Sky deals with difficult subject matter with remarkable skill, grace, and poise. This collection is an experiment of affects which questions addiction, identity and belonging in a deeply captivating manner. Carrick-Varty fuses personal memory and individual lyrics with Greek and Buddhist mythology. The poems are wide-ranging in scope and tone: replete with lyrical wanderings and wonderings that allow for audacious leaps of image and colliding realities.

JAN | CARCANET | £11.99 | PBS PRICE £9.00

ALEC FINLAY: PLAY MY GAME
REVIEWED BY SHALINI SENGUPTA

The opening poem in Finlay's collection, 'questions & answers', explains poetry with poetry. It is – like most of the poems in *Play My Game* – endlessly captivating and always slightly out of reach. Finlay's work is at once an experiment with language and the relationship between image and text. The shapes of his poems introduce a different kind of visuality and push the possibilities of poems on the page.

FEB | STEWED RHUBARB | £10.00 | PBS PRICE £7.50

ATAR HADARI: GETHSEMANE
REVIEWED BY LEAH JUN OH

In an empathetic arrangement of "the Jewish voices which often escape the gospel narrative", Hadari seeks the Semitic foundations, cultural norms, and customs underpinning the New Testament. Hadari unfolds social, legal, and intellectual counter-gospels in rhyme and rhetorical catechism: from world-weary Herod, to Saul on the road to Damascus. *Gethsemane* is a conjuring of characters that speak in voices wise to, unaware of, or kindly ambivalent to any significance of the times.

JAN | SHEARSMAN | £10.95 | PBS PRICE £8.22

LEDBURY CRITICS TAKEOVER

KATIE HALE: WHITE GHOSTS
REVIEWED BY SHALINI SENGUPTA

Hale's debut is unflinching, vulnerable, multilayered. It traces maternal lines of inheritance and takes us through legacies of slavery and whiteness in an ambitious reach into history and the sonics of past archives that lie "dormant at the heart of the house". Hale uses the lyric with sophisticated inventiveness to create webs of fractured political narratives. This accomplished debut innovatively critiques and celebrates the ghostly capacity for language to deconstruct the given.

MARCH | NINE ARCHES PRESS | £10.99 | PBS PRICE £8.25

YANG LIAN: A TOWER BUILT DOWNWARDS
REVIEWED BY SHASH TREVETT

With an introduction and cover by Ai Weiwei, this is Yang Lian's twelfth collection with his long-term translator, Brian Holton. An important poet of the Misty School (banned in China), his poems "grow in the direction of both life and death" (Ai Weiwei), dwelling on the pandemic in Wuhan and the erosion of democracy in Hong Kong. Containing poems rich in image and metaphor, this masterful translation won a PEN Translates award.

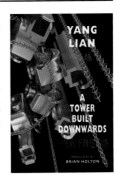

MARCH | BLOODAXE | £14.99 | PBS PRICE £11.25

L. KIEW: MORE THAN WEEDS
REVIEWED BY MAGGIE WANG

Kiew's debut *More Than Weeds* grows in the literal and metaphorical gaps between languages. The poems span two broad and overlapping categories – botany and the author's Chinese-Malaysian heritage – and many use white space to offer multiple ways of reading. Kiew works deftly with sound ("Rain has flushed thought / as dust off five-pointed leaves.") and image ("so many caterpillars are stripping / green tissue, denuding stems.") and surprises the reader with metaphor: "don't talk to the street trees / they aren't from here".

FEB | NINE ARCHES PRESS | £10.99 | PBS PRICE £8.25

BOOK REVIEWS |

MAGGIE MILLNER: COUPLETS
REVIEWED BY SHALINI SENGUPTA

Millner's amorphous story-in-verse reckons with what it means to upend conventional ideas of intimacy and loss. Endlessly innovative and captivating, this collection resists transparency; the speaker always holds a little something back while demanding recognition of validity and humanity. Millner's poetic subject is more concerned with becoming known to herself – within the sensorium of the poems – than being known. This wildly intelligent, shapeshifting collection is a joy to read, both at the level of line and thought.

MARCH | FABER | £12.99 | PBS PRICE £9.75

JACOB POLLEY: MATERIAL PROPERTIES
REVIEWED BY MAGGIE WANG

Material Properties strikes a rare balance between intellectual complexity and stylistic accessibility, inspired by a series of Old English riddles from a tenth-century codex known as *The Exeter Book*. Each "riddle tests and challenges, / laying open to the raw / my being, which is always / with other beings in the world," he writes. The same could be said of his poems: reading them may be like dreaming, which "is a kind of worry, yes, and a / flower, happening as it does / in the dark."

FEB | PICADOR | £10.99 | PBS PRICE £8.25

YOUSIF M. QASMIYEH: EATING THE ARCHIVE
REVIEWED BY SHASH TREVETT

Qasmiyeh's second collection returns to Beddawi Refugee Camp with renewed intensity and an elasticity which allows the lines to breathe with each break. Here are new poems about the camp: about his siblings; about patience, words and silences; the home and the poet's mother and father, met with a new familiarity. These are tender "memorials" for "a future subject to many pasts" written with a precision which invites the reader to travel alongside a living archive.

FEB | BROKEN SLEEP BOOKS | £12.99 | PBS PRICE £9.75

Christopher Reid Toys/Tricks/ Traps

Reid's hypnotic and whimsical meditation is an investigation into Wordsworth's famous adage: "the Child is father of the Man". Reid's lines run away with themselves: they appear to be in free fall in a manner that gives the sense of poetry without limits. The poet, however, is never afraid to dive into the centre of the crisis. Across the collection, the poems probe the extremities of power and violence in ways that unsettle and grip the reader's attention. Reid's poetry remains playful, lyrical, interrogative, and observant.

FEB | FABER | £14.99 | PBS PRICE £11.25

Suggesting a curious fascination with the problematic aesthetics of "art for art's sake", Singer's meticulously crafted *Artifice* ventures to answer the question, "To what end"? Carefully wrought from Folios, from the oddments of artists, sculptures and historical crevices, Singer replicates classic artefacts in poetic form. Exquisite and intricate, *Artifice* weaponises concision with masterful restraint; each brushstroke thoughtful, each word intentionally placed.

MARCH | PROTOTYPE | £12.00 | PBS PRICE £9.00   **LAVINIA SINGER**

Across the collection, Stevenson's poems appear as unforgettable vignettes that emphasise, in her words, "the craft, coherence and architecture" of her oeuvre. Poems like 'The Women' and 'To My Daughter in a Red Coat' are poignantly stratified explorations of the self in conversation with the natural world: a theme that is part of Stevenson's enduring legacy and bears testament to the formal range of her writing. This is a key volume for anyone interested in modern British women's poetry.

FEB | BLOODAXE BOOKS | £25.00 | PBS PRICE £18.75

BOOK REVIEWS

SPRING PAMPHLETS

LISA BLACKWELL: HOW IT WILL HAPPEN

How It Will Happen is composed of a series of prose poems which tell the story of a woman's life. The poems covering her youth are loaded with tension; we know we are heading towards "it", but we do not know what "it" is or when "it" will come. Yet these growing-up poems, as with the rest of the pamphlet, are deep and richly detailed in themselves. Encompassing the dark as well as the light, this is a full and fervent portrait of a life.

How it will happen
Lisa Blackwell

MAYTREE   PRESS | £8.00 |

MARTIN FIGURA: SIXTEEN SONNETS FOR CARE

Commissioned for the Social Care Day of Reflection and Remembrance, Martin Figura's *Sixteen Sonnets for Care* commemorate those who gave so much during the darkest days of the pandemic. Written with tenderness and empathy, this is a deeply moving record which gives voice to the vulnerable and all those "faces stricken behind masks". Through heart-breaking poems such as 'Fifty Masks' and uplifting vignettes like 'We are here', Figura offers a sincere tribute to everyone working and living in social care.

FAIR   ACRE   PRESS | £7.00 |

CALEB PARKIN: THE COIN

The poems in Caleb Parkin's *The Coin* are largely in tribute to mothers, with specific references to Parkin's own mother and grandmothers, and moving pieces about a family in crisis as their mother battles with cancer. Parkin's poems contain gentle humour and often delightfully surprising language, as in 'To The River Stour': "you wiggle like an idyll". Visiting also themes of class and place, *The Coin* is an excellent addition to Parkin's accomplished body of work.

THE COIN
Caleb Parkin

BROKEN   SLEEP   BOOKS | £7.99 |

FIONA SMITH: TRAVELLERS OF THE NORTH

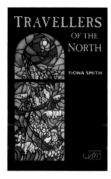

In *Travellers of the North*, Fiona Smith pulls the Irish saint Sunniva out of the murk of mythology and grounds her in reality as an accomplished voyager. Smith's taut verse and use of dialect deftly conjure Sunniva's journey as the reader travels with her, over the sea and through language. Words from Ireland, Shetland, Orkney, and Norway appear, following Sunniva's route, and the Irish saint is truly "translated": from myth to reality, from Ireland to Norway, and from the page to our consciousness.

ARC   PUBLICATIONS | £7.00 |

KANDACE SIOBHAN WALKER: KALEIDO

Kandace Siobhan Walker's dextrous double pamphlet offers an innovative take on the tarot's Major Arcana. Mirrored in its entirety, *Kaleido* sits "between two selves", interweaving familiar archetypes from The Hermit to The Heart, with existentialism, fast cars and noisy bars. In the face of "Radio silence from my spirit guides", Walker forges a visionary language of "kaleidoscopic awareness." This is a compelling debut for all those seeking new direction(s) in life.

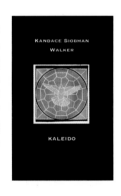

BAD   BETTY   PRESS | £10.00 |

SAMMY WEAVER: ANGOLA, AMERICA

Taking its name from a prison in Louisiana, *Angola, America* is the worthy winner of the 2021 Mslexia Pamphlet Prize. This astonishing debut immerses us in the world of the inmates and offers a powerful statement on the prison system. Weaver re-examines the horror of [exhibit : electric chair] and confronts the criminalisation of race: "my whiteness permits / my witnessing". Each poem carefully weighs atrocity and empathy, challenging and re-humanising: "both man / & beast, broken-boned & returned to their cages."

SEREN   BOOKS | £6.00 |

SPRING BOOK LISTINGS

Sanddancer by J E Neary

The kitchen in our old home
was tangerine warm,
checkerboard tiles laced with
the ghost of whatever you made last Sunday.
Was it muffins or madeleines?
I told the kids at school
my mam can speak Spanish y'know.
I wanted them to see you like I do -
the sanddancer,
bold and bright,
like I am running home
sodden with the rain,
knowing you have a soft towel
warmed through on the radiator for me,
and I can't wait to tell you everything.

Poetry Book Society

M Community
METRO Takeover

Metro worked with the Poetry Book Society to run a
poetry competition with the theme of 'Home' as part
of our Metro Community Takeover programme.